Word Vomit

Dani L Smith

For Amy. For having the patience to listen.
Over and over.

CONTENTS

CONTENT WARNING

This book contains strong language and themes of a sexual nature.

swipe for: two best friends that toy
with your emotions

you make me want to
dust off my heart
and attempt to love again.

when someone comes along and somehow works their
way into your heart… it completely takes you by surprise
but makes absolute sense. loving again after so much
betrayal and heartache is another step forward.

you make me feel
so safe.

and i'll keep you safe
in return.

your touch
sets off fireworks
underneath my skin.

you've reawakened my heart and the sparks fly every time we're together. when we touch, my skin is left tingling hours later.

i knew i would crush on you again.
i just didn't expect it to be
so sudden
and so intense.

just when i thought i was over it, all the feelings came back
and hit me like a ton of bricks. i just can't seem to quit
feeling for you.

your smile
brightens my soul.

i could be having a horrible day and one smile from you
can turn everything around.

i'm learning to love again
thanks to you.

you've captured my attention. you have my morning thoughts and evening dreams. your presence, our interactions, your friendship… slowly, i have felt my heart fluttering and opening up once again. thank you. whatever happens, you've shown me that i am capable of trusting and loving someone again.

you're all motorbike leathers,
dark chocolate and coffee.

WORD VOMIT

your scent
brings comfort
to my soul

the cards
the birds
the symbols
the energy in the air.
it's all shifting
changing
changing
changing
telling me to take control
and tell you how i feel.

can't you feel it too? the energy shifting, the signs appearing. signs sign signs everywhere, screaming at me to tell you. tell him tell him tell him.

even my dreams are
reaching out for you.

WORD VOMIT

dreams
constantly seeking and searching
finding you
arms reaching out
and you falling into them
where you belong.

i could drive for hours
with you by my side.

so let's go driving
anywhere and everywhere
peas in a pod
needing no one but each other

bruise my lips with kisses.

forgive me, for when we talk my eyes always fall upon your mouth. as your words touch my ears, i long for the passionate touch of our lips. hungry, starving, needing that connection. leaving us both bruised and sore and sheepishly smiling.

WORD VOMIT

how does it feel
to be one of
my favourite men in the world?

WORD VOMIT

are your eyes even open?
do you see me?

this one-sided shit
needs to stop.

WORD VOMIT

today i realised
that you're not just a machine.
you have feelings and emotions.
your sparkling eyes and pink face,
cute little smile and safe energy.
the opposite of an automaton.

i forced myself to go on a date.
but once again,
he wasn't you.

that's the problem... they're not you.

i've worked myself
into quite the
predicament with you.

i don't know which way to turn or which way to go. the only thing certain is my feelings for you, an uncertain person.

everyone sees it,
our chemistry.
everyone tells me,
get together.
everyone says,
you're a great match.
everyone,
but you.

there's a spanner in the works and it just so happens to share the same name as you.

it took me so long to realise
that you are my safe place.

WORD VOMIT

my safe space
and yet not my safe space.
my mind soother
and yet my mind mangler.

your voice
reverberates around my soul
leaving an imprint
on my spine.

truly the best feeling when the hum of your voice sends
vibrations through my entire being.

you want attention from those that can't give you what you
need.
a genuine, warm love.

WORD VOMIT

let me love you in the way that you deserve.

you want what you don't need
and you need what you don't want.

tell me, my love. who is more guilty of this? you - focusing on things and people that don't deserve a second of your time. or me - foolishly waiting around for you to see sense and realise that i've been here all along. what a pair.

i will always remember
that feeling i had
when i realised that i loved you.

a sudden realisation that it's not just a crush and my
feelings for you are real.

WORD VOMIT

i live for the day
that i can my fingers
through your hair.

sometimes it feels like my life is on pause... waiting for
that moment you wake up and realise that i'm what you
want in your life.

i'm standing right here
waiting for you to realise
how much i care
and want to be with you.

forever waiting for you to either wake up or open your
eyes.

you say i'm interesting, weird, and
one of the best people you know.
yet you won't make that first move.

sigh. you say all of these things, cause my heart to sing, and i'll always be left waiting.

even the cards
are screaming at me
to tell you.

the cards screamed at me to tell you what was in my heart.
even though the feelings weren't mutual, i am glad to have
shared a piece of my soul with you.

well
you were worth a shot.

i will never regret telling you how i feel. i'm glad i got it out in the open and i'll never have to wonder what your response would have been. you were worth a shot and you always will be.

your jealousy is
jarring and
unattractive.

enough said. you can't live your life trying to control others and working yourself into a bad mood. take a step back and reassess your priorities.

don't you know that
mixed signals aren't fair?

don't you know that you can't have your cake and eat it, too? you think you can dangle a carrot in front of me and i'll keep attending to you, but honey that is not how the world works. shame on you.

absence makes
the heart
grow **stronger**.

WORD VOMIT

you were gone for so long and my heart grew strong.

being reunited with you
is like finding that
missing puzzle piece.

WORD VOMIT

before i met you
and since then
whenever we're apart
i often feel incomplete
and only whole again
when you're by my side.

all it took
after months of being apart
was just one look
for me to fall in love with you
all over again.

WORD VOMIT

just one look
that's all it took

i felt it,
things shifting between us.
unable to tell yet,
if it'll be good or bad.

i wrote this after i hadn't seen you for so long
months later, i still can't tell if the shift was good or bad
enlighten me, please.

i bet i can make you laugh
more than she can.

i'm always second best.

how can you
go back to her
knowing the result
will be the same?

WORD VOMIT

you fool
don't do it
it ended
for a reason

ladies
do not let a man
treat you like a girlfriend
only to draw
friendship lines
between you.

i always have trouble following my own advice.

i can't complete
with your gorgeous past
and stunning future.

i'm haunted by inadequacy over what once was and what could be.

who are you trying to convince...
yourself
or the world?

WORD VOMIT

you exhaust me with your hot n' cold behaviour.

foolish boy,
i could never forget you.

WORD VOMIT

i still remember
your words
that i "seemingly"
forget you're around
and i just shook
my head and laughed
because darling
you are simply
unforgettable

i love you, flyboy

hahaha i'm such a fool for you. terrified of your gaze upon these words yet unable to quit these feelings. would you believe me if i promised that i was trying to? it might be awkward for you but it's even more so for me. do you think i enjoy your lack of reciprocation? because i sure as hell don't. here comes the beginning of letting go.

i'm tired of going on dates
with people that i have zero chemistry with
meanwhile there are two men in my life
one unobtainable
one not interested
whom i have scorching chemistry with.

find someone who matches your energy and effort
because starting off-balance will leave you
feeling empty in the end.

my date kissed me.
it felt forced.
he went in for a second.
i turned away and grimaced.
he's not you.

that's the thing about all of these dates… none of them are ever you. i'm not even sure if that's a good thing or a bad thing anymore. every day i get to spend with you just leaves me with more questions. every mixed signal you throw my way just sends my brain into a spiral. they're not you. they never will be you. but i'll never have this with you.

i have my answer.
so why can't i stop
these feelings for you?

WORD VOMIT

your smile
is too enticing
i can't resist
your face

i need to stop wasting my energy on men who are
unobtainable or not interested.

i'm always scolding myself for wasting time on the pair of
you, but to be honest you're my favourite way to waste
time and energy.

dear heart,
when will you accept
that he isn't the one for you?
he just sees you as a friend,
so stop pining over someone
who has painted you
a very clear picture.
love, brain.

WORD VOMIT

dear brain
lesson learned
love heart

another guy
another date.
the same whispers,
he's not you.

and he
never will be.

don't let his
drips of attention
keep you trapped
under his spell.

WORD VOMIT

all i want to do
is embrace you
and never let go.

why do you get so upset
when you learn
that i've been on dates?
you gave me your answer.
you can't have your cake
and eat it too.

and tell me
in light of recent developments
what will you do
when you find out
that your friend had the balls
to ask me out
instead of you?

today you hurt me.
that's it.
you hurt me.
i can't even begin to describe it.
it just hurt.

WORD VOMIT

a blow to my soul
like no other

apology accepted.
i could never stay mad at you,
you make me smile too much.

WORD VOMIT

no matter what
kind of mood i'm in
you always manage to tug
the corners of my mouth

despite being hyper-aware
of this unrequited situation
i still can't convince myself
to stop loving you.

but i suppose that's okay
because while i will always love you
i've accepted that i can love others
just as much.

oh look
another disappointment of a person.

i really hoped - i really thought - that you wouldn't let me down. but guess what? i was wrong again.

tell me you don't care
one last time.

WORD VOMIT

tell me again
so that maybe one day
i'll finally believe you
and you'll be left wondering
where you went wrong.

don't go back to her.
have a new beginning with me.

i scribbled this down months ago, but it's quite interesting
that this week seems to have brought me a new beginning.

it's sad when one of your best friends
expects you to change your behaviour around them
just because they're interested in someone
and they don't want that person to see how close you are.

our friendship has blossomed
since i've been able to
shelve my feelings into
the right place.

why are your eyes still so
magnetic after all this time?

swipe for: a three-timing ginger manager

lover, let's just
sit back on the couch,
my head on your shoulder,
yours resting on mine,
my fingers in your beard,
hands entwined.

poetry is so versatile
for i wrote this about one person
but now it relates to another.

tell me your fears and woes
and i will vanquish them
to make way for your hopes and dreams.

WORD VOMIT

tell me everything you wish
and i will smite the bad
yet warm the good

you were orbiting
on the edge of my life
for months
and now you're here
front and center
pulling me in.

i know you've been burned
but baby so have i,
so put your hand in mine
and we'll embrace the fire together.
the girl with the phoenix tattoo
and the guy with flame-kissed hair
reborn again, starting anew.

vibrant
you make me feel like a million colours
the world, my world,
is much more clearer
and vibrant
with you in it.

like my own
personal kaleidoscope

two leos
a rabbit and a dragon
fireworks guaranteed.

totalitarian
the shadows of your past are illiberal beings
let's walk this dystopian future side by side.

inconceivable
i thought loving you
was inconceivable
but here you are
proving me wrong.

WORD VOMIT

your smile
is infectious.
a contagious virus
that we keep passing
back and forth
to each other.

i guess
you could say
i'm lovesick

having you in my life
lets me see a thousand colours.
you're my own personal kaleidoscope.
a cornucopia of pigment.
loving you in technicolour.

all it takes
is your presence
your searching gaze
a lingering smile
and a quick wink.

and oh
i love it when i see you from afar
and watch you scan the room for me
a homing beacon for your soul.

if you're King of the clouds
would you make me your Queen?

and i still have the video
of you mouthing this song.
one of my favourite memories
of a connection still ajar.

in three weeks
you have given me
so much more
than he did
in almost two years.

and you disappointed me
so much more than him
in a similar space of time.

your problem?
mixed signals. inconsistency.
my problem?
loving you despite it all.

foolish me

you are so violent
with my heart
and careless
with my feelings.

just once i'd like someone to be gentle with this soft heart
of mine.

rewind to last month
play.
you saying that you'd never hurt me.
fast forward to now
play.
you've forgotten that i exist.

rinse and repeat
this vicious cycle.

his forgetfulness
does not define you.
don't let it steer you
just because he can't make up his mind.

WORD VOMIT

i don't know why
i let you treat me this way.
i might as well
change my name to "doormat".

and it's such a shame
that we allowed rumours and hearsay
to ruin something good
and instead of talking
we each turned inwards
and away from each other.
spiteful, unhappy people
were the cause of our downfall
masking their efforts
by pointing the blame at us.

WORD VOMIT

don't draw back so much
that i'm left wondering
where you went
or what went wrong.

love is a lot like gin.
a bad one burns
but a good one
warms the soul.

tip your head back and swallow

sorry.
i don't believe in friendly ghosts.

you went from codename keith to codename casper in a
short space of time. ghosting isn't fucking cool.

no wonder
you couldn't remember
the things you said
at night.
you were busy
copying and pasting it all
to two or three
other girls.

don't expect me to make you a priority
when i've only ever been an option for you.
don't think i can't sense the change in your vibe
and your lack of attention to what we were building.
don't think i don't know that i'm not the only one in your
inbox
because you just can't help but love the attention.

did you really
think i wouldn't
find out
that you're a player?

and to those that spread this utter fabrication
did you really think that i wouldn't find out the lies that fell
from your vicious, toxic lips?
karma is a bitch
and it's coming for you.

do not listen
to unsolicited advice
from miserable, jealous people.
listen only to your heart.

WORD VOMIT

i learned the hard way
not to listen to malicious lies
because it sabotaged something
that could've been great.

originally i slammed the door
but since discovering these fabrications
i have an urge to open it ajar
and hope to find you peering back at me.

i need to keep my cards close to my chest with this one
for fear of manipulation from those that would like to see
me fall.

dear heart,
give me a break.

WORD VOMIT

just this once
deliver me something
or someone good

swipe for: a two-timing boy who
fancies himself a princess

the first time i heard your voice
it felt like i'd broken into a thousand grins.
it was like a homecoming.

WORD VOMIT

on monday we matched
tuesday, a three-hour phone call
we kissed on our first date on wednesday
thursday, we flirted and chatted
friday, we talked travel
i missed you on saturday
second date on sunday
mario kart, scary games,
and a heated moment on your living room floor.
the seven days of you.
and what a week it was.

kiss me until the world disappears.

don't quit on me now.

i knew even before our first date
that you would leave a beautiful
mark on my life.

a beautiful mark on my life and my body
you cracked me open and showed me i could love again.

i fell for you fast and hard
even though i didn't say so.

damned if i do
and damned if i don't
a catch-22 of feelings
and admitting to them.

it's okay
if i can't tell you how i feel
then at least i can scream
my feelings for you
into the void.

because i've built these walls up
where love can't reach me
and i'm so scared
to breathe life into what i feel
so i'll write it all down
paint pictures with my words
until i find the courage
to ask you to be mine

the look on your face that evening
guitar hero in your living room
the light catching your eyes in a certain way as they
searched for me.
that's when i knew i'd fallen.

i knew you'd be nothing but trouble
and you never proved me wrong.

you told me to stop looking at you that way
to stop trying to read you.
you were terrified, weren't you?
because in that moment i read you completely
and i knew you'd break my heart.

we've all been there. we've looked too closely into a fuckboy's eyes and known they would waste our time and chip off a piece of our heart, yet we still stuck around to see how it played out. dear reader, know that your worth is beyond what emotional vampires in your life deserve.

WORD VOMIT

when you say you miss me too
do you even mean it?
or are you just parroting
because you think it'll earn you a treat?

and just this once i would like someone to look at me and mean the things they say instead of letting words slip out of their mouth just to get their leg over.

endearing
you inspire me
to be a better person
a better version of myself.
but is it worth it
when you don't even notice
the end result?

WORD VOMIT

i just want you to see me

i hate this feeling of uncertainty
but baby, i love it when you call me.

not knowing where you stand with someone is a pretty rubbish feeling. if they cared, they'd make time. stop listening to their words and pay attention to their actions. a busy person will still make time for the one one they love. if they're not doing this, then they're not the one.

according to you
the right way to deal with a miscommunication
is to make it even worse.
bury your head in the sand
ignore the questions and messages
and in the end destroy what we could've had.

indestructible
everytime i rebuild myself
i think, this time i'm shatterproof
but it's all ephemeral.
over time, i've learned that it's okay
to have a fragile heart
as long as i have an enduring soul.

you will suffer great damage
from all these games you play.

catastrophic.
need i remind you
that karma is a bitch
and you can't play a player?

monstrous
it's frightening, what i do to myself.
always loving more, but somehow
becoming misshapen in the process.

WORD VOMIT

i always give without expecting anything in return
you claimed yourself lucky
because it led us to each other
but where are you now?
maybe it's time for me to finally be selfish.

it's saddening to know
that probably in the exact moment
i took a photo to send to you
and tell you that i miss you
was when you were
departing my life
and breaking my heart.

let me know
when you have time and space
for me in your life.
until then
i'll have my phone on loud
waiting for a text
that you'll never send.

thank you for the souvenir
across my wrist ♥

and thank you for the lesson
to never give so much of myself away
to someone that doesn't know how
to care for anyone but himself.

i guess you're saving all
the kisses and
heart-eye emojis
for the other girl.

why hide the truth? honesty is key when it comes to relationships, because the people involved will know where they stand. trust is part of the foundation to successful connections, so don't shatter someone's belief in you.

ferocious
i bet you're so proud
of the games you play.
but honey, don't you know
that lions can bite?
don't be fooled
by my silence
because these claws
will rip you apart.

just because i am sedate
it doesn't mean that i'm
not watching your approach
wary of your next move.

let me get this straight.
you can leave me on read for three days
but i can't leave you unread for seven minutes.
is that right?

please stay just a little longer.

tell me
was it all just embellishment
to get what you wanted
or was it real for you?

i gave you every opportunity to be honest
to admit that you were seeing others.
i wouldn't have been mad, i just would've known where i
stood
but you still chose to lie
and that… that, dear, set my rage on fire.

i don't think it was a coincidence
that on the day i cleansed myself in a spiritual waterfall
you decided to leave my life.

and what a cleansing it was to finally be rid of your
presence.

i called you out on your shit
and you decided to remove yourself
from my life.

and at the time it stung
but honestly
thank you
for taking out the trash.

you showed me that i could love again
but you also proved to me that no one wants to love me in
return.

the ones that came after you
have also supported this theory.

you aren't even all that
to be playing these games.

and you aren't even worth the drama
so keep writing your shitty blog posts
and i'll carry on with my shitty poetry
because honey, remember, you just can't play a player

i told myself that i wouldn't check my phone for your reply
i'd turn it off and leave it be until later.
but on the coastline of tintagel
i found myself wondering
and switched it back on.
no signal.
but that was the sign i needed
to prove that i didn't need you.

i guess i just wanted to thank you
for opening up the hard shell that my heart had become.
too bad you didn't want to stick around
to watch me blossom.
too bad for you
obviously.

when did my self worth become so low
that i will allow a guy to treat me
the same way that others in my past have
but i'll still nod my head and crave their attention.

i just can't move from this beach
looking out to sea, tintagel castle across the way
i can't move until i've gotten all the words out
how alive you made me feel
the heart you reawakened
the calm sense of familiarity i found within you
broken paths leading us to each other.
and the boulder that crashed through
separating you from your consideration for me
you stared into the chasm
threw your hands in the air
and walked away.
which leads me to where i am now
on the edge of this cliff
knowing you'll never catch me if i fall.

pray thee, who are you
to enter my life
and reawaken this old dragon's heart
just to dash it against the very cliffs
that i serve to protect?

WORD VOMIT

the rumbling in my chest
is the stirring of my heart you have caused
the smoke escaping
is the warming of my feelings
the moment you had the prize
you escaped with fistfuls of gold
and left my castle in ruin.

just another cowboy
with a southern accent.

the universe knew i needed to come to this magical place
because you plotted to deplete me of all my energy.
so here i am, surrounded by goddesses
and an eerie sense of serenity
recharging myself and starting anew.

am i crying
or has the wind
gotten to my eyes
on this cliff face?

so many people visit this place with their loved ones
yet here i am, allowing the wind
to blow away the ghost of you.

blowing away the ghosts of your past shouldn't just be for romantic relationships. toxic friendships, family members and general acquaintances need to be cast aside and scattered away into the wind. your peace of mind is worth so much more than negative people.

you're so far removed now
and i think that's where i'd
like you to stay
so i'll cast the memory of you
off this edge with my tears.

swipe for: an "honest" ginger who
does nothing but lie

you met me at the airport
after only a week of messages
circling around
until we spied each other
kissing, squeezing
and your hand on my thigh
hands down one of the most romantic things
i've ever experienced.

the airport kiss
the squeeze of my hip
your hand inching up my leg
to grasp my fingers
glancing at each other
through the window's reflection
inside the elevator
an immediate pounce
lips meeting, hands all over
your fingers inside of me
mine wrapped around you
hand-holding and tickling fingers
as we talked over the table
your arm thrown around me
a kiss planted on my head
my hand in your back pocket
outside of king's cross
resting against a wall
your fingers on a mission
during our open conversation
desperate kisses at departure
until we meet again.

i could spend the whole day
jumping tube trains
and dodging into empty lifts with you.

don't fade into a fond memory.
my heart is yours for a place to stay.

WORD VOMIT

i can't wait to lock the door
and pretend the world doesn't exist
for an entire weekend with you.

and it couldn't have been better.

your grip, your touch
it's something that i crave
whispers in my ear
lips on my skin
you've awakened something
i long thought was dormant.

and whether it's for a moment or forever
whether we come crashing back together
or ricochet in different directions
i'll always treasure what we had.

i'm tired of sleeping
in a bed
that's too big
for only me.

and take me back
to last week
on your single air bed
your arm thrown over me
your face snuggled into my shoulder.

i fell asleep to the sound
of your heart beating.

the purest sound and feeling
at your most vulnerable.
wrapped up in your arms
and held so tight.

you twitch and jerk in your sleep
as if you struggle to relax.
just let go
i'll catch you if you fall.

but who will catch me when it's my turn to fall?

conversations with my mother
he's intelligent
"you have two degrees and you're worldly aware."
he's positive
"you're textbook positive."
he's confident
"as are you most times."
he's inspiring
"when you think about doing something, you go for it and
don't look back."
he's beautiful
"you are very attractive."
…
"tell me again why you aren't on his level."

never again will i doubt myself
over a boy that can look me
dead in the eye and lie.

you're the first thing on my mind
and the last when i go to sleep.
but do i even cross yours at all?

WORD VOMIT

i wanted you to love me in your own time
but whether it was distraction on your end
or my laid-back attitude
things just didn't go how i wanted.

i want you
in my bed
hand on my ass
kissing my neck

and who am i, to stand in the way
when opportunity comes knocking for you?
and maybe i am foolish for saying that i'll wait
but my heart works in its own special way
for you are worth every nanosecond to eternity.

you are destined for great things
i just wish you'd invited me along for the ride.

months later i've realised
that it's okay
because great things have also come my way
and you don't deserve a taste of them.

i told you i was falling
and asked if that messed everything up
you said not everything
you just didn't want to fall at a slower pace.
but we both know it's because
you don't think i stand out.

once upon a time
i said you were destined
for great things.
but in reality,
you're only destined
to be a jerk.

WORD VOMIT

i know that i'm not your priority
and i know that i'm a fool
for thinking that an option like me
could be worthy of an upgrade

undeniable
it's undeniable that you hurt me
and irrefutable that you broke me.

"is there someone else?"
"no."
i could smell your lie
from 236km away.

don't kid a kidder, don't play a player, this is a bullshit free zone.

you knew what he did to me and how it made me feel,
but that didn't stop you from doing the exact same thing.

these boys i come across
are all the fucking same. "i'm different than the others,"
they're not. "i'll always be honest with you,"
they lie.
yet their transgressions are as
vapid as their egos.

WORD VOMIT

you watch all my stories
and like my pictures.
i have you on mute
because i know you're
still with her
and you're only interacting
with me because
you want me to see.

WORD VOMIT

it's a flaw that i'm very much aware of
no matter how terrible a guy treats me
i will still leave the door open
in case he wants to return again.

the moment i see him
lick his lips
i brace myself for
the impact of his lies.
the glance in the wrong direction
the shift in position
collision imminent.

this kind of tic would be foresight into becoming collateral damage.

you're so ensconced
in the idea of being kinky
that you completely forget
how to properly please a woman.

too many people are obsessed with the idea of being kinky in the bedroom so that they can metaphorically wear it as a badge of honour. yet they lack the ability to please their partner(s). what a shame.

puzzling are the minds of those
that think they can pick someone
back up where they left off and
expect that person to drop everything
for them. when they left with no
warning or discussion, thinking
that the person will want them in
the same way. then they become
upset and gaslight when they realise
the person learned their worth
and won't give them another moment
of their time. puzzling are those minds.

WORD VOMIT

you came back to break me
and you almost succeeded
but i rose like a phoenix
and flew into true love's arms.

and it was the one
after the one after you
that showed me true pleasure
and selflessness both
inside and outside of
the bedroom.

WORD VOMIT

you call yourself an honest sinner
but sweetheart, i know your secret
you're nothing more than a lying hypocrite.

swipe for: miscellaneous dalliances

i liked the way he
grabbed me with fierce intensity
and passionately kissed me,
pinned against his wall,
his hands all over, towering over me.
my bag dropping to the floor.
no time for the coffee he made
or an apartment tour,
just our desire to touch
and come together.

WORD VOMIT

when we laid in your bed
and you told me the meaning
behind the black bands
tattooed around your arm,
that was when the foundation
of the walls i've put up
started crumbling.

i tell myself every time
"don't fall for this one"
but with him
i looked in the rear-view mirror
and was honest with myself.
"you're going to fall for him, anyway."

this modern love is terrifying
worrying if you mean the things you say
or if you'll jump to the next temporary quick-fix.

i rarely wrote about you
for fear of jinxing your presence.
of course it didn't matter
as you lied and left anyway.
but thanks for the writing inspiration
in the wake of your transgressions.
much appreciated.

assumptions are interesting
for the guy i believed to be relationship material
turned out to be a fuckboy
and the guy i thought would be a fuckboy
turned out to be relationship material.

i wish people would
tell me what i'm doing right,
instead of what i'm doing wrong.

it's all about the negative things lately. there's no construction to it. no rhyme or reason. there's no focus on the positive. just tell me what i'm doing right for a change.

i'm always expected to listen to others
but no one listens to me.

tell me your problems and i will help you unfold them all.
but where are you when i need you to unfold mine?

WORD VOMIT

i still don't know how
to write about you
you captured my heart
but you wasted your chance.

you will always be a chapter that i cannot write down.
there could've been so many pieces about you. but... you
wasted your chance so why should i waste my energy on
how terrible you made me feel in the end?

i said i'd wait for you
but i didn't say i'd be celibate

WORD VOMIT

i feel bad for you
because you could never handle me.

spiritual
don't trust someone
who speaks nothing but
transcendent lies.

your holier than thou pompous attitude and fabrications
are not welcome here.

i always fall for boys
that don't have the balls
to tell me that they're no longer interested.
instead they let me find out
their fucking transgressions
and finish the puzzle myself.

a good man will never keep secrets from you or keep you guessing. he will be honest and loyal to you and the relationship you have with each other. to all the men that did nothing but disappoint me, both inside and outside of the bedroom: thank you for being so awful that i could forget about you.

i crave being outside
naked and on the ground,
in the sand, in the grass, in the mud,
rolling in mother earth,
or draped in a tree,
or lounging in a rock pool.
my mouth full of freshly squeezed juice,
vegetables, fruit, produce of the earth.
rubbing leaves between my fingertips,
wildflowers in my hair,
the sun kissing my strands,
and the breeze stroking my skin.
salutations and stretching.
away from this mundane life
and one with nature.

take me away from this stressful life and let me just live
outside, one with Mother Nature.

i always trust
the wrong people.

i've learnt a hard lesson. that i can only trust myself.

stop caring
about people that don't care about you.

three "relationships" in five months.
it's time for me to enter a waiting period
and focus purely on myself.

my third heartache of the year
broke my ability to feel.

WORD VOMIT

romantic soulmates
are so archaic
for i have found mine
in my best friend.

once upon a time
i said my abuser was the best
sex of my life.
due to recent experiences
i would like to withdraw
this statement.

it feels good to be able to correct unhealthy thoughts.
and i know the best is still yet to come.

if someone does not bring a shred of positivity
into your life, then do not waste another
ounce of energy on them.

WORD VOMIT

never let a man
ruin your lipstick,
eyeliner or mascara
unless he is kissing
or throat-fucking you.

go ahead.
treat them how they treat you.
in no time at all
they will question you.
and then you can respond,
"now you know how i feel."

in the past, whenever i have given men the same shitty treatment they have given me, they have pissed and moaned about it. obtuse to the fact that how they're feeling in this short moment is how they were making me feel all along. so don't be afraid to give the crappy person in your life the same crappy treatment they give you. they'll either shape up or you can shop them out. sail away, hun.

you can't pin me down
i'm the wind in your hair
water in your hand
the grain of sand on your skin
a fireball before you
unwilling to stand still
pin me down, i dare you to try.

too many people in my past have tried to be clever and attempt to control me. contort me into their vision of who i should be or force-feed me their opinion like a sip of vinegar. don't try to change people whose entire being is something you can't even begin to comprehend. don't try to change people, period.

feelings change and people change. i used to have a nasty habit of letting men that have wronged me have a second chance... or third... and i was always the one hurt in the end.

long gone are the days where i waste myself on people that cannot reciprocate. people that don't even have the decency to show you one shred of respect do not deserve yours in return. cut the toxic people out of your life and watch how good you start to look.

it's all a little bit more painful
and exaggerated in words.
but that's the magic of poetry
isn't it?

to all the boys who think these pieces are about them...
treat women better.

ABOUT THE AUTHOR

Dani L Smith is a UK-based author born in 1988 who uses poetry and pieces of writing as an outlet. She shares and engages in her content online.

In her spare time she enjoys reading, travelling, road-trips, and spending time with her loved ones.

Her debut poetry book, *Hildr Fragments*, touches on her experience in abusive relationships from 2006-2016 and her miscarriage in 2016.

You can find her on Instagram: @danilsmithpoetry

Printed in Great Britain
by Amazon